Contents

Introduction

Following the success of '200 Tricky Spellings in Cartoons', I've been asked by parents and teachers to produce a similar resource for children of primary school age. Enthusiastically, I set about collecting a new set of tricky words. Ten months later, here it is - a compilation of over 160 hints for 264 new spellings with colour illustrations.

Is this book for my child?

This book is not a structured spelling programme. It does not replace any part of a child's current literacy instruction at school. It complements it to help equip the children with additional ways to remember tricky spellings.
It's suitable for children who:
- prefer to learn by seeing and doing
- have tried traditional spelling strategies (e.g. Look, Cover, Write, Check, and breaking words into sounds and syllables) but with limited success
- continue to confuse similar sounding and similar looking words
- have dyslexia or other specific learning difficulty.

How mnemonics work

About 30% of English words can't be spelled using phonics. Their spelling patterns have to be memorised. Children might initially spell *what* as *wot* and *eight* as *eit* and later *ate*. But if we help them identify patterns within words, for example break *what* into *w* (the first sound) and a phonetically regular word *hat* (w + hat), the spelling becomes easier to recall. In order to consolidate memory for the new spelling, why not act it out with the child: *What? A hat? What hat? Oh, I've got one on my head... How did it end up there? What?? A wind blew it over?* While many children in Reception and Year 1 will learn tricky spellings using traditional methods with no trouble, some will continue misspelling them beyond late KS1 and KS2 - these children may benefit from the helping hand of mnemonics.

Mnemonics (pronounced with a silent front letter *m* [ni'monic]) are memory triggers that help us remember things we easily forget, for example telephone numbers, left/right directions, and tricky words. Children and adults enjoy using mnemonics because of their funny and unusual associations with things. They provide humour that often helps learning and supports long-term memory. What's more, mnemonics require almost no effort to learn.

About the mnemonics in this book

Most mnemonics in my publications are in the public domain - they are widely used by teachers, parents and grand-parents, and people with dyslexia. They are shared and handed down from one generation to another. Stylistic variations exist but the underlying ideas have remained unchanged for years. For this reason, it is virtually impossible to trace the exact origin of a particular mnemonic in order to accurately reference it.

Many spelling hints in this book are suggestions I received from readers who contacted me after they'd enjoyed '200 Tricky Spellings in Cartoons': primary school teachers, teaching assistants, dyslexia practitioners, and parents. I am very grateful for all the fantastic ideas, which I successfully use in my own dyslexia support practice.

This book doesn't contain every tricky spelling a child will encounter in primary school, only some of the most common ones. As I continue receiving suggestions from educators and parents, there will be a part two to this publication that will make the spelling mnemonics bank more complete, if that is ever possible.

How to use this book

Help the child find the tricky word in the index at the back of the book. Read the short text together and ensure the child's understanding of the spelling hint. Don't forget to have fun exploring the visual hints and story lines. Talk about similar familiar situations so the child can relate to the idea. Help them turn their experiences into a new funny or silly story that links directly to the mnemonic. Mnemonics work best when they are personal.

It's important to refer back to the newly learned mnemonic later the same day and in the following days using fun activities that will ensure memory consolidation. Focus on action and play while combining as many senses as possible during learning: use pretend-play to act out stories and situations, encourage visualisation, and experiment with fun voices. Always focus on the 'tricky' part of the word: *How **did** you remember it?* Below are suggestions you might find useful.

Ask the child to write the word:
- on the fridge/freezer, windows and glass patio doors using a wipeable marker (make a rule no other markers are allowed to avoid permanent damage)
- on the pavement using coloured chalk
- on the ground or fence using a squirty water bottle
- in shaving cream on the table, or spread the shaving cream on the surface so the child can use their finger to write the word
- in a baking tray filled with a shallow layer of salt or flour using their finger or a wooden spoon.

Help the child to:
- mould the word out of plasticine or dough
- make the word out of small building blocks
- bake the letters out of pastry or cookie dough, arrange them in the right order, and then enjoy eating the word.

Encourage the child to:
- recall the spelling mnemonic while bouncing on a trampoline or sofa (if allowed)
- say the tricky part of the word in a funny voice, different accent, or a singing voice
- draw a picture/poster with the word and display at home or school.

The best way to learn is to teach: ask the child to teach tricky spellings to other family members and their friends.

I hope you will have lots of fun!

Lidia Stanton
lidia.stanton@icloud.com   in https://uk.linkedin.com/in/lidiastanton   f https://facebook.com/dyslexiaideas

Copyright note

Intellectual Property Office (2014) *Exceptions to Copyright: Guidance for Creators and Copyright Owners.* October 2014. Newport: IPO. Pp. 5-6.

what
what hat?

when

hen

Wh**en** did you get up, **hen**?

As early as the cows.

Wh**en** will you go to bed, **hen**?

I'm so tired, about now.

who
wicked hairy ogre

why
why hate yogurt?

Bleah!

Why hate yogurt?

It's good for your bones.

It's good for your gut.

It comes in lots of flavours.

And it can be frozen!

here
where
there

Here
every
rainbow
ends

Where?
here

There?

Not t**here. H**ere.
See? W**here** the gold is.
My gold!

The word 'here' hides inside 'where' and 'there'.

how
on wheels

Did someone say *sausages*? Yum!

But what about Dad? **Does** he like them?

No, **d**ad **o**nly **e**ats **s**andwiches.

does

does Oliver eat sausages?

Oliver is 5 today. Next week I will be 8.

I need something that I like
to give to my good mate.

I wonder... does Oliver eat sausages?

one
only one?

Only **on**e sausage for me?

Only **on**e star for my picture?

Only **on**e left?

Yay! **O**nly **on**e day till the holiday!

Mr and Mrs
Mr Red and Mrs Red Socks

Mr Red was like no other man; he was red.

But his wife had no colour when they wed.

"My dear wife, here's a present in a box."

And that's how she became Mrs Red Socks.

want

ant

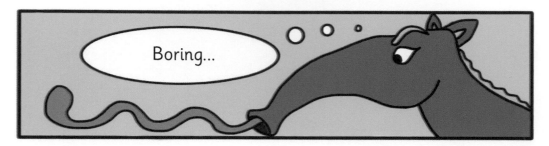

I w**ant** an **ant**.

You can't snack all day.

I don't w**ant** to eat.

I w**ant** to play!

said

Who said dancing is silly?

Snakes and insects dance.

Sally Ann is dancing.

Smart Alec is dancing.

And I dance!

because

Not many people know that

big **e**lephants **c**an't **a**lways **u**se **s**mall **e**xits,

and that

big **e**lephants **c**an't **a**dd **u**p **s**ums **e**asily,

but everyone knows that

big **e**lephants **c**an **a**lways **u**nderstand **s**mall **e**lephants.

moth**er**
moth

A **moth** sat on the lamp.

And made my **mot**h**er** jump.

Noooo!

My **mot**h**er** cried out, "Noooo!"

And swallowed the **moth** whole.

school
super children a-choo!

Super children go to school.

Secret code word is 'A-choo'.

If you ever hear 'A-choo!',

That's a super child at school.

you

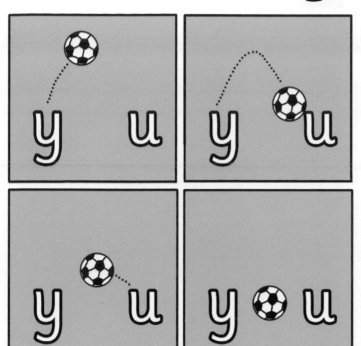

Is it true no one can beat **you** in football?

Yep! It always kicks the ball when no one is watching. What a sporty word...

oh

Oh, hello!

Oh, hello!
Here you are.

all (-all)
a lost lesson

The **tall** teacher in the h**all**

called **all** players by the w**all**,

and gave them a b**all** so sm**all**,

it went up but didn't f**all**.

And that was **all**...

ate (-ate)

A d**ate** on a pl**ate**

for a pir**ate** and his m**ate**.

But who **ate** it first

and who was too l**ate**?

-ea
I eat my tea by the sea

Each year I eat my tea on a beach by the sea.

A healthy feast instead of beans or cheap meal deals.

I reach for wheat bread with cream spread, lean meat and peas.

Pears and peaches - a real feast to say the least.

-ght
good hiding trees

These are good hiding trees

at night

and when it's light.

The tree on the right might look rather slight

but it's a good hiding tree all right.

How many elves are hiding in the trees at night?

-ould
oh, you (u) little duck

Could you cross the pond? **O**h, **you** little **d**uck.

Would you hurt your legs? **O**h, **you** little **d**uck.

Could I be your friend? **O**h, **you** little **d**uck.

I sh**ould** help you then. **O**h, **you** lucky **d**uck.

-ous
to us

Is Mr Wilson humor**ous**?
T**o us**, he is.

Are roads danger**ous**?
T**o us**, they are.

Did Milly look nerv**ous**?
T**o us**, she did.

Is Mrs Morris gener**ous**?
T**o us**, she is. Very!

-ough
oh, you (u) grumpy hippo

Oh, **you** **g**ippo,
en**ough** with feeling blue.

You might be r**ough** and t**ough**
but you just won't pass thr**ough**.

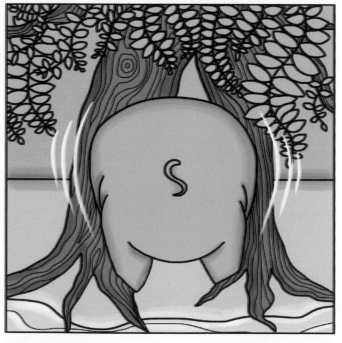

Stop pushing your hardest, don't
pl**ough** thr**ough** the poor tree.

Squeeze under the low b**ough**
and walk around it. See?

sure (-sure)

Would you like to find a hidden treasure? **Sure**!

Great job! Will you play again? **Sure**, Coach. My plea**sure**!

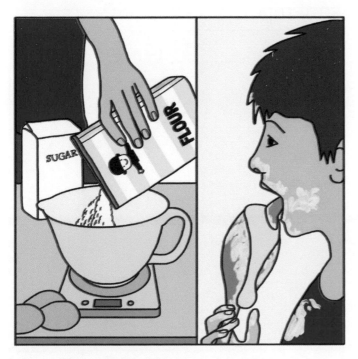

Could you help me mea**sure** flour and sugar? **Sure**!

Finally some lei**sure** time. Let's eat ice-cream. **Sure**.

-ture
today you (u) are (r) epic

You've drawn the best pic**ture** and made the best sculp**ture**.

You've remembered the 'e' in temp**era****ture**.

You haven't frac**ture**d your knee in football.

You've listened to the na**ture** in the forest.

You've taken your little sister on an adven**ture**.

You've learned not to tor**ture** little garden crea**ture**s. Ever!

Today U R Epic!

You haven't broken your sister's building blocks struc**ture**.

You have a shining fu**ture**, my boy!

one

only one elephant

two

two twins

three

three feels free
(but the first sound is different!)

four

four people in our family

five

five vests

for every day of school

six

six helps to mix

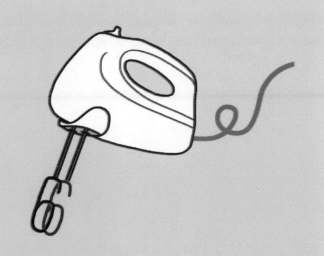

to fix a yummy dessert

seven eleven

seven rhymes with eleven

But have you noticed they are not even numbers?

eight

eight good hiding trees

You'll struggle to find me!

nine

nine feels fine

Sometimes it feels dev**ine**!

ten

ten men

One would do just fine
on the toilet door, B**en**!

twelve

tw**elve elve**s

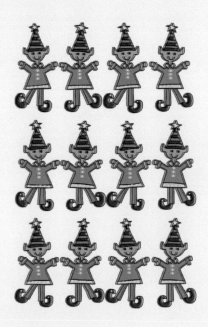

twelfth

tw**elf**th **elf**

The tw**elf**th **elf** is just one **elf**
when you spell it.

thirty

thirty is rude

Don't be so sh**ir**ty, th**ir**ty!

forty

forty is naughty

It has kicked off its 'u'!

fifty

fifty is funny

If only fi**f**ty wasn't so wi**f**ty, it would be the funniest stand-up comedian.

thousand

th**ous**and grains of **sand**

To **us**, a th**ous**and feels like a truck load of **sand**.

Some words have eyes...

see

seen

look

eyes

peek

peer

peep

and ears inside them.

Every day at school,
I h[ear] and I l[ear]n.

I w[ear] my [ear]rings on my [ear].

What if the [Ear]th had an [ear] and could h[ear] us? It does.
But it doesn't have a mouth to tell us to be kinder to her.

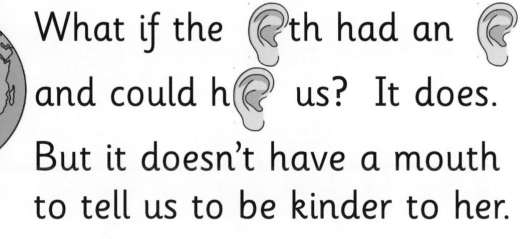

Bob's b[ear]d is from [ear] to [ear].

advise or advice?
Is it a snake or a cat?

Meet **S**nake, an active animal that **s**lides in a **s**erpentine motion. It **s**imply never **s**tops!

And here is **C**at, a **c**omfort **c**reature that doesn't want to be active when it doesn't have to be. **C**at is **c**omfy.

Snake and Cat have important jobs to do when it comes to spelling. One is doing a lot, the other... nothing at all.

verb
doing word

noun
non-doing word

to advise

When you advise someone, you do it actively by speaking or writing to them.

the advice

But a piece of advice (or the advice) is given to you without you having to lift your finger.

to practise

I would like to practise law. It's a lot of hard work but the money is good.

a practice

I imagine my legal practice (the building) in the town centre. It stands there waiting until I grow up.

to license

Adults license their cars by filling out forms.
To license something is to get permission to use it.

a licence

A paper licence is not doing much in someone's hand. But it allows the adult to drive a car, or open a bar.

to devise

Our teacher devised a way to count all of us as we come into the classroom.

a device

The little electronic device rests in his hand every time the break is over.

affect or effect?
action or result?

My cat's napping **a**ffected my school grades. I could never get up to do homework!

Guess who's not allowed to play out after tea now?

One person's (or cat's) **a**ction **a**ffects the behaviour of the other, which brings a r**e**sult, or **e**ffect.

I'm sure you can help me with maths, Snowflake.

Think of RAVEN

Verb = doing word
Noun = non-doing word

R Remember
A Affect
V Verb
E Effect
N Noun

aloud or allowed?

a
loud
orchestra
uses
drums

allowed
low

Why are **low** flying planes not al**low**ed in built-up areas? They create 'noise pollution' for people and animals.

Some military planes make the ground shake!

angle or angel?

ang**le**
glue

Did you check the an**g**le before you **gl**ued the picture to the wall?

Why do an**gel**s always look beautiful?

angel
gel

They use a lot of hair **gel**. There are some rebels, though.

bear or bare?

bear
ear

Why are my **ear**s so small?

Polar bears have small **ear**s to avoid losing heat. They stay warm in very cold climates.

Why does the barman tell feet to take off their shoes before serving them in his bar?

bare
bar

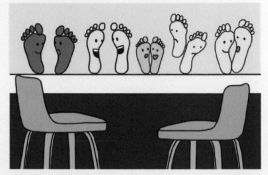

So they can't argue they are all right!

berry or bury?

What looks like a b**e**rry but isn't?

berry
cherry

A ch**e**rry, which is a fruit. B**e**rries don't have stones but lots of seeds in their skin.

Why do dogs b**u**ry their bones **u**nderground?

Because no one else will do it for them.

bury
underground

break or brake?

break
easily

Hands up everyone who breaks things easily!

Always brake when you see a rake!

brake
rake

cereal or serial?

real
cereal
corn

Cereal, such as corn flakes, is made from real corn.

serial
series

Serial numbers follow one another in series.

Why was six afraid of seven?

| 0006 | 0007 | 0008 |
| 0009 | 0010 | 0011 |

Because seven ate nine.

compliment or complement?

compliment
i like

I like compliments but **I** blush and **I** don't know what to say.

"Your singing is lovely."

"Oh, no. It's really awful. **I**... **I** mean... Thank you."

complement
complete

Butter completes bread - the two complement each other.

Other matching pairs are:
- fish and chips
- strawberries and cream
- Batman and Robin

Umm... Your turn!

currant or current?

currant
ant

I'm pretending I'm a currant!

This is not going to end well, is it? Get out, or you'll get eaten.

current
river

Did you know that some river currents can be turned into electricity? How exciting!

dairy or diary?

dairy
air holes

Is it really mice that make **air** holes in cheese?

Who knows? The history of d**air**y seems to be full of holes.

How do I know Gregg Heffley likes comics as much as I do?

i
a m
reading

I am reading 'D**iar**y of a Wimpy Kid'.

deer or dear?

deer
eerie

How can d**eer** live in **eer**ie forests and yet be so timid?

Dear
earphones

Let's not play hide and seek. I need to h**ear** that song again and you need untangling.

Love, Becca x

desert or dessert?

de s ert
sand

Why don't pirates ever get hungry on de**s**ert islands?

Because of all the **s**and which is there.

sandwiches

de ss ert
sweet stuff

My favourite **s**weet **s**tuff has to have strawberries in it:
- **s**trawberry **s**hortcake
- **s**trawberry **s**ponge
- **s**trawberry **s**cone
- **s**trawberry **s**wiss roll.

fair or fare?

fair
air

It's not **f**air Tom was longer in the **air**!

Being suspended on a broken wheel for hours is not fun, Sid.

This **fare** will take you **far**!

fare
far

May I have a **fare** that will take me **far** enough to miss the vets today, please?

grate or great?

grate
rat

What do g**rat**ers and **rat**s have in common?

They both like cheese.

great
eat

It's gr**eat** to **eat** your favourite food!

Eat, not play with your food, Mario.

heal or heel?

he**al**
alright

Is your finger he**al**ing **al**right?

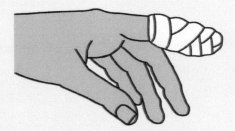

Hard to tell. I haven't had my game console in my hands since Friday.

h**ee**l
elegant

Mum has two **ele**gant heels.

One foot looks better in high heel shoes, the other in low ones. Does she not limp? Yes, she does, but **ele**gantly.

new or knew?

What do you call a brand **new** t-shirt?

never
ever
worn

What do you call a bad day at the BBC?
Nothing **n**ew to report.

knew
kicked

I **k**icked myself because I **k**new the answer.

not or knot?

What do these DO **NOT** signs mean?

Clockwise: do not enter; do not use phone; do not feed birds; do not run; do not touch.

knot

What's a pretzel?

Bread in a **k**not.

lose or loose?

lose

Mum complains my oldest brother is not good with money:

"If money could talk, his would only ever say "Goodbye"...

Why are Betty's two front teeth **loo**se?
She thought candy floss and dental floss were the same thing. But there is something that keeps her **loo**se **tee**th together. It's **too**thpaste.

mail or male?

snail
mail

male
Alex

Did you know that 'sn**ail m**ail' actually exists in the real world?

Letters that we drop in a post box are called sn**ail m**ail.

Some names are both m**ale** and fem**ale**. Take **Ale**x. When you hear about a baby called **Ale**x, you don't know if it's a boy or a girl.
Can you think of other names that can be both m**ale** and fe-m**ale**?

meat or meet?

meat
meat
eat

I like to **eat** **meat**.

meet
meet
gr**eet**

Grrrrr!

But I don't like to m**eet** and gr**eet**!

one or won?

only
only
one
on earth

Isn't it amazing there is **on**ly **on**e of you **on** earth?

Can you **w**in it?

'One' or 'won'?
If you can **w**in it,
it has a '**w**' in it.

pair or pear?

pair
air

This **pair** of trainers makes me fly in the **air**!

pear
eat

When I **ea**t a p**ea**r I feel full because it contains fibre. I then don't crave sugary snacks. I love to **ea**t p**ea**rs!

pea**ce** or pie**ce**?

pea**ce**
pea

Peas are the most **pea**ceful of all vegetables. "Make **pea**ce, not soup" is what they say to grocers.

pie**ce**
pie

What's Grandma's favourite advice? "Have a **pie**ce of **pie**!"

plane or plain?

plane
lane

Do planes use lanes?
Yes, they follow invisible spots
called coordinates. They don't
fly in straight lines but from one
spot to another.

plain
in white

The bride looked
lovely but Ben
thought he
looked plain
in white.
Cheer up, Ben.
Stop looking down
in the mouth.
It's a wedding!

peek or peak?

'No peeking', said Mum just as
Pete peeked into the oven
to see what was cooking.

'Not eels in leeks again!'

'Why did Pete flee so fast before
dinner?' wondered Mum.

peak
A

Some letters look like things
in the real world.

The letter A looks like a ladder,
angle, alligator's mouth, duck's
beak, and a peak!

see or sea?

see

I'm a ninja!
No, you're not, Dad.
Ha! Did you **see** me do that?
Do what?
Exactly!

sea animals

Can you draw four other sea animals?		

seen or scene?

seen

How do you know carrots are good for you?

How?

Have you **seen** a rabbit wearing glasses?

crime scene central

Why did Mr Potato call the **C**rime **S**c**e**n**e** **C**en**t**ral line?

His wife wasn't in the same room when he saw a neighbour try ketchup on chips.

some or sum?

some money

sum of numbers

$$2+7=9$$

Here's some money, Tom. Just remember I'm not a bank and money doesn't grow on trees.

That's not true. Banks have branches!

Why are you doing your maths on the floor, Julia?
The teacher told us not to use tables.

To sum it up, numbers are no fun for Julia.

son or sun?

son
boy

"Who's Mummy's little boy?"

sun
fun

We run and run, having fun in the sun. Summer has begun!

stationary or stationery?

Ahoy, Matey.
Ye want t'be station**a**ry?
Anchor the ship then, **a**rrrr.

We asked a hundred people to name an item of station**e**ry.

Ninety nine said **envelope**.

threw or through?

thr**ew**
Ew!

Mum thr**ew** away Theo's old trainers.
"**Ew**!" was all she said.

Can **hippos** pass thr**ough** obstacles without pl**ough**ing them down?

oh
u (you)
grumpy
hippo

Not if they are **grumpy**!

Also see page 24.

there or their?

there
here

Start with **here**.
If it's not **here**,
it's over t**here**.

Where?
Over t**here**.

Also see page 7.

their
girls
dirt
shirts
skirts

The g**ir**ls got d**ir**t on the**ir** sh**ir**ts and sk**ir**ts.

I'd like to be in the**ir** school!

or they're?

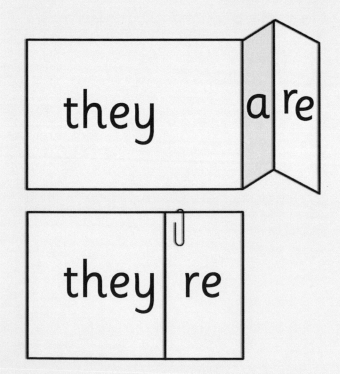

they

a re

they re

Think paper clip,
think apostrophe.

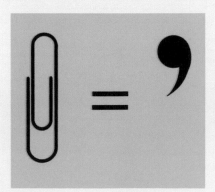

you're means **you are**

too or two?

too cool

two twins

Can anyone be **too cool**?
This guy can.

When he walks by, people get chills and his fans get brain freeze!

There can only be **two twins**. One, two. **Two tw**irling and **tw**isting **tw**ins.

wait or weight?

wAit
4
it

I'm watching my sister take a selfie.

Wait for it... (**WAit 4 it**...)

What's the wei**ght** of **g**ood **h**iding **t**rees?

good
hiding
trees

Heavy. Twelve elves are hiding in them!

weather or whether?

weather
sea

What's the weather at sea like today?

The weather at sea is not looking good. A storm is on its way.

whether
he

Whether he wanted to or not, he had to made a decision...

whose or who's?

whose
nose

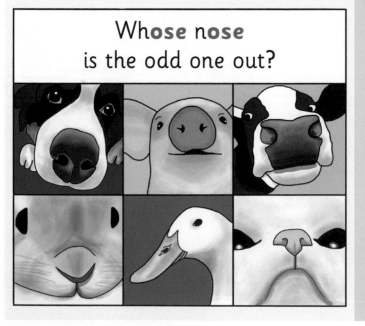

Whose nose is the odd one out?

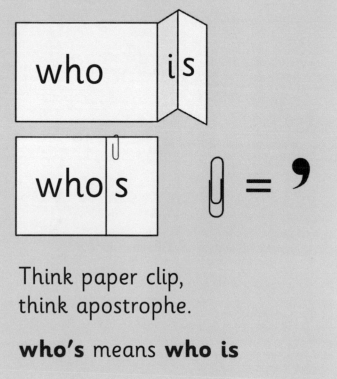

who | is

who | s

◊ = '

Think paper clip, think apostrophe.

who's means **who is**

witch or which?

wit
witch
itch

Why do **wit**ches cackle?
Because they are **wit**ty.

Why do w**itch**es ride on broom-sticks?
Because they have **itch**y feet.

wh

wh**at?**
wh**o?**
wh**ere?**
wh**en?**
wh**ich?**

Which is yet another question that starts with '**wh**'.

your or you're?

your = you®

If something **belongs** to some-one, you will say to them "This is your _____".

The '**r**' at the end of 'your' is there just like the trademark sign Ⓡ is placed after a name that **belongs** to an organisa-tion. Ⓡ says: "This brand is ours. It **belongs** to us."

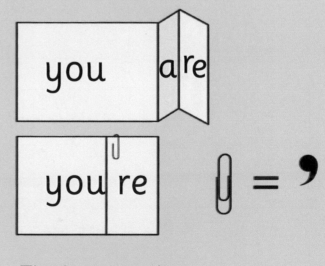

Think paper clip, think apostrophe.

you're means **you are**

Letter sandwiches

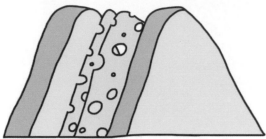

inte**re**st

May I int**ere**st you in sandwich making?

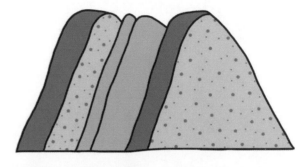

every

Every sandwich needs a filling.

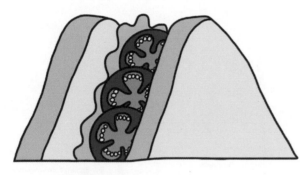

f**ollo**w

Follow your nose and see what you can find in the fridge.

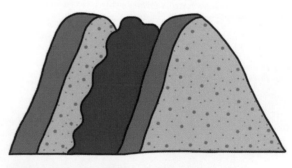

e**ve**n

Does the jam look **eve**n on each side?

56

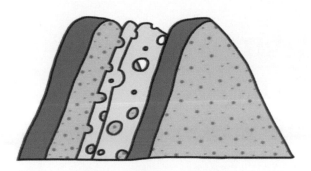

a w a y

Don't throw any cheese **away**.
Put an extra slice in.

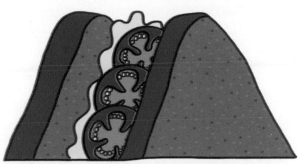

diff ere nt

Why not make your sandwich
diff**ere**nt? Use brown bread.

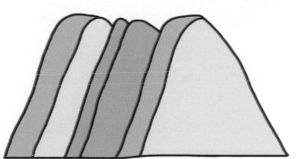

b ette r

Are two slices of ham b**etter**
than one?

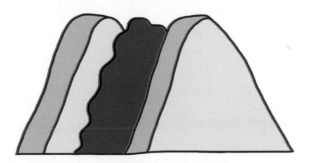

def i n i te

Now, this sandwich is
a def**ini**te winner!

again

again
Britain
rain

What happens in Brit**ain** ag**ain** and ag**ain**?

R**ain**...

amateur

The boys' acting made it the best **amateur** production ever performed in this theatre.

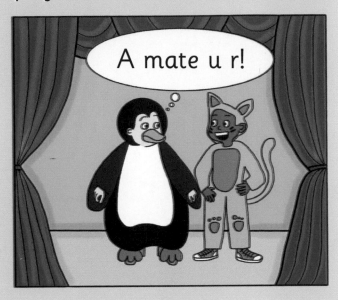

A mate u r!

athlete

exactly
ten
events

A decathlon athl**ete** has to compete in **e**xactly **t**en **e**vents.

balloon

Balloons are **ball**-shaped **loon**y inflatables. Did you know they are scared of just one type of music?

Pop music!

beautiful

b ig
e ars
a ren't
u gly

Big **e**ars **a**ren't **u**gly.
They are **beau**tiful.

Always **be a** beautiful girl
inside and out.

bicycle

uncle
bi**cy**cle
icy

Don't ride your bi**cy**cle when
it's **icy**.

Yes, Un**cle Cle**o...

blue

What should you do when you
see a blu**e e**lephant?

Cheer him up!

build

You and **I** (ui)
will build
a house.

After you've
done your
homework,
boys.

Oh,
Muuuum!

busy

busy
bus

The **bus** was so **bus**y I finally had a chance to be a stuntman!

care/scared

are
c**are**
sc**are**d

I know you **are** sc**are**d, Bella. I'll be very c**are**ful listening to your heart. I'll take good c**are** of you.

church

ch   ur   ch

Put 'ch' on the left
and 'ch' on the right,
and you are (**ur**) in the middle.

com**pet**ition

com**pet**ition
pet

When **Pet**al has won again, her owner **Pet**unia declared: "The only real com**pet**ition is a **pet** com**pet**ition."

down

down
low

Down! Low on the floor.

Owen trained his **ow**ner to smile every time he stayed l**ow**.

easy

egg
and
spoon

"The **egg a**nd **s**poon race is so **eas**y", said Ed a moment before he was disqualified for using both hands.

daughter

dear
Alice
u (you)
got
hairy
toes

We all have hairy toes but the hair is so small we can't see it.

Dear Mum, so do you!
Alice x

design

de**sign**
signature

A good de**sign**er always puts a **sign**ature on their de**sign**s.

family

father
and
mother
i
love
you

Mum and Dad loved Ben's **family** picture.

fascinating

fascinating
sleeping
cats

Sleeping **c**ats are fascinating.

But don't touch Pebbles' nose. Cats lose appetite if their sense of smell is upset.

fasten

fasten
going fast

Fasten your seatbelt, Snuggles.
We are going **fast**!

first/bird/birthday

first
bird
birthday

I got my **fir**st **bir**d on my **bir**thday. Her singing **irr**itated the neighbours but th**eir** cat was a real fan!

friend

i
fri**end**
end

> I, till the **end**, will be your **fri**end!

girl

"That **g**irl **i**s **r**eally **l**ovely", thought Jake...

girl
is
really
lovely

until he saw her pick her nose at lunchtime.

innocent

in
no
century

In no century was crime treated as something **innocent**.

know/knight/knee

know
knight
knock
knee

Do you **kn**ow why **kn**ights never look scared even when they tremble with fear?

They **kn**ock their **kn**ees with silent **k**s!

laugh

Duke's joke was so good Adam had to enter him in a pet talent competition.

laugh
and
u (you)
get
happy

lightning

There is no 'e' in ligh**tn**ing. Just see what happened to it!

light/ning

listen

listen
ten **songs**

On Saturday, Joe lis**ten**s to **ten** songs from the Top **Ten** Chart.

little

teeny **t**iny **little** **e**ggs

What do you think might have happened in the bird's nest?

ne**ces**sary

It's ne**ces**sary for Billy to put on one collar (**c**) and two socks (**ss**) when he gets ready for school.

— 1 collar

— 2 socks

o**cca**sionally

O**cca**sionally, Billy plays rugby. He puts on an extra shirt - he now has two collars (**cc**) but only one sock (**s**).

— 2 collars

— 1 sock

nei**gh**bour

our
nei**gh**bour
giant
honey
bear

Tilly! **Our** neighbour is a **g**iant **h**oney **b**ear!

not**ice**

ice
not**ice**
pol**ice**

POLICE NOTICE

Are you ready for **ice** on the roads? Slow down and expect delays. Do not drive unless it is necessary.

Pol**ice** issued a not**ice** about **ice** on the road.

now

nw

There's no better time than n**o**w - unless it's the time to get up.

ocean

only
cats'
eyes
are
narrow

Did you know? Sea otters are called 'the cats of the **ocean**'. They are cute, playful and enjoy wrapping up in seaweed when taking long naps.

often

out of ten

I **often** score my pranks out **of ten**.

Creeping up on my brother with cymbals is ten out **of ten**! Even if I'm not allowed to do it more **often**...

out

O U Trouble!

Oh, you trouble. **Out** you go!

Pebbles gave no comment...

people

pe**o**ple

People live on the Earth and the round planet (**o**) lives in the spelling of the word 'pe**o**ple'.

present

sent
present

When she **sent** the pre**sent**, the red post box couldn't open its mouth wide enough to keep the ribbon and bow neat.

That's why pre**sent**s are best **sent** from the post office.

queen

queen + **u**mbrella

q + **u**

You will never see the **qu**een without her **u**mbrella.

When you write a 'q', always follow it with a 'u'.

rhythm

rhythm
helps
your
two
hips
move

How do you tell if a tissue has **rhythm**?
You put a little boogie in it.

shoulder

shoulder
should

Well done, Shaun! You **should** pat yourself on the **shoulder**.

Also see page 22.

sign

sign
signal

A **sign** is a kind of **signal** that tells us what to do.

surprise

burp
surprise
rise

Bobby **burp**ed all night. It will be a sur**prise** if we see him **rise** early.

weird

weird
we
awesome

Yes, **we** are **we**ird. Yes, **we** are a**we**some!

wood/would   young

w**oo**d

You won't confuse w**oo**d for w**ou**ld when you imagine two w**oo**d logs inside the word.

Think w**oo**d, think logs.
Think w**ou**ld, think a little duck (see page 22).

"**You** are so **you**ng, child...", thought Grandad.

If you've enjoyed this book, you can find more fun spellings here:

accept/except	challenge	grammar	parliament
accident	committee	hair/hare	persistent
accommodate	commission	heritage	pharaoh
achieve	debt	hiccup	pharmacy
adapt/adopt	definite	hierarchy	physician
address	dilemma	hole/whole	possesses
answer	discipline	honour	prejudice
anxiety	embarrass	immediately	principle/principal
apparent	emigrate/imigrate	independent	privilege
appear	engineer	irresistible	professor
architect	ensure/insure	island	pronounce
argument	environment	issue	pronunciation
bargain	equipment	jealousy	publicly
beginning	exaggerate	knowledge	queue
believe	excellent	leather	quiet/quite
biscuit	familiar	manoeuvre	raspberry
board/bored	February	medieval	receive
brain	flour/flower	message	recommend
brilliant	foreign	misspell	recover
broccoli	fortunate	money	resource
business	garage	noticeable	restaurant
calendar	ghost	occurred	sausage
Caribbean	government	opportunity	schedule
cemetery	graffiti	parallel	scissors

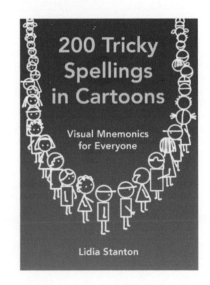

200 Tricky Spellings in Cartoons

Visual Mnemonics for Everyone

Lidia Stanton

separate	tomorrow
significant	touch
special	vicious
success	village
surface	villain
than/then	watch
together	Wednesday
theatre	wrap

Index

Printed in Great Britain
by Amazon

23536527R00041